Gothic Art

Petrus Christus (d. *ca* 1473)
St. Eloy in his Workshop
Oil on Wood
Lehmann Coll. New York.

Gothic Art

PEEBLES ART LIBRARY **Sandy Lesberg, Editor**

First published 1974
by
Peebles Press International
U.S.: 140 Riverside Drive, New York, N.Y. 10024
U.K.: 12 Thayer Street, London, W1M 5LD

ISBN 0-85690-033-8

Illustrations provided by:
Giraudon, Paris: pages 9, 10, 13, 14, 15, 16, 17, 18, 19, 20, 21, 23, 24, 25, 26, 27, 29, 30, 34, 35, 36, 37, 38, 39, 40, 41, 42, 43, 44, 45, 46, 47, 48.
André Held, Lausanne: pages 3, 8, 11, 12, 16, 19 (lower), 22, 28, 31.
Scala, Florence: pages 32, 33.

Distributed by
Walden Books, Resale Division in the U.S. and Canada.
WHS Distributors in the U.K., Ireland, Australia, New Zealand and South Africa.

Printed and Bound in Great Britain

Introduction

'An Age of Transition'—when shall we ever come round to restricting the term 'Middle Ages', whose generally accepted meaning is quite ridiculous, to the period that saw the death of Joan of Arc and the birth of Christopher Columbus? This was an age in which the West underwent the greatest upheaval in its history after that which ushered in the so-called 'Middle' Ages with the barbarian invasions of the fifth and sixth centuries; in which the work on the last cathedrals was completed—though some, such as that of Batalha, were to remain forever 'unfinished'—and the building of mansions and palaces began. A town such as Bourges, which at the time of Charles VII was the capital of the province of Berry, today owes its fame to the House of Jacques Cœur rather than to its magnificent cathedral; and after all, is not St Peter's in Rome a palace rather than a church?

This period of transition, like every age that gives birth to something new, is both fascinating and painful to watch. It is particularly fascinating and fruitful for the art historian: through this study by Michel Hérubel the wealth of European painting in the fifteenth century is revealed in all its splendid glory. In reading the following pages, one soon gets the impression that during this period painters of genius were one of the commonest of human types. Future historians may well say the same of the end of the nineteenth century and the beginning of the twentieth, but the great names of our own era have all been associated, to a greater or lesser extent, with Paris, while in the fifteenth century one meets excellent artists throughout the whole of Western Europe, from the Loire Valley to Poland, from the plains of the Low Countries to the Italian peninsula.

However, in order to study their works, one must consider their places of origin, and these, one finds, have much in common. Florence, Basle, Avignon are all towns. The large commercial towns are also artistic centres in which great painters live and work. One might call them the birthplace of the artist, in the pure sense of the term, since from now on this word, previously unknown, begins, though still not in current use (it is only in the eighteenth century that it takes on the full meaning that it holds for us today), at least to define a social reality, an individual who performs a type of activity which brings him recognition and admiration. Art and the artist become inseparable from an urban background, we can even say from a middle-class background in which 'works of art' are bought and sold. Whether it be Barcelona, where, in 1487, Huguet received payment for the six panels of the St Augustine Altar-piece *which he painted for the Tanners' Guild, or Bruges, where Memling was employed by the Council of Nine, everywhere the city inspires and supports the artist, and commissions his works. Even the concept of 'civilization' can no longer be dissociated from its etymological origins—*civis, civitas.

This in itself is sufficient to differentiate the fifteenth century from the age of feudalism with its powerful nobles backed by their vast domains, and also from the classical era of the French monarchy. The ideals of feudalism are summed up in the words 'courtly' and 'courtesy', which imply everything one could wish for in the way of polite behaviour, delicate manners and lofty sentiments. But these terms are derived from 'court', which then meant the court of the castle, whether of Ussel in Corrèze, or of Troyes or Poitiers. In the days of feudalism there was no distinction between the capital and the province, town and country. When the era of the monarchy arises, only one court is recognized, only one palace. The word 'court' then provides us with 'courtier' and 'courtesan'. Etymology is certainly revealing.

These social developments during the 'mediaeval' period naturally produced fissures which, looked at from a distance, in many ways resemble geological eras formed by periodic eruptions which produce mountains and continents. In this case the mountains are frontiers and the continents nations. Born of war, they never cease to be devastated and remade by war. Western Europe consists of a number of hostile blocs, each wishing to assert its independence and exert political and economic power. Even the Turkish advance into Hungary and as far as the walls of Vienna failed to evoke any sense of unity—for the East and the West likewise formed two mutually hostile blocs after the fateful year of 1453.

During the period in which these enormous upheavals were taking place, effective power and authority were to be found only at the level of the town, with its merchants, its bankers, and its craftsmen's guilds. Such were the towns of Flanders, Italy, and in Eastern Europe the Hanseatic League, whose ships crossed the oceans or sailed along inland waterways from the Baltic to the Adriatic. In this time of troubles, the Duchy of Burgundy alone retained a sufficiently large territory and sense of unity for the ducal court, whether at Dijon or Lille, to remain an enduring centre of attraction. Moreover, the patronage of the Dukes of Burgundy exceeded by far that of a Jean de Berry or a Louis of Anjou.

The places which gave birth to these artists and, more important still, those where they carried out their work, are also revealing: Bruges, at once a ducal capital and a merchant city, compared with Florence, the city of the Medicis, for its bankers with princely ambitions. Equally significant are the movements of artists from place to place, for painters travelled widely. Though England and France, which were at war and therefore somewhat isolated from the rest of Western Europe, remain a little outside the main stream, the travels of the great painters follow the main trade routes: from factories of the Hanseatic League, along the Rhine and other German rivers, to the cities of Tuscany and the shores of the Adriatic. Memling, born near Mainz, brought up perhaps in Cologne, and later a citizen of Bruges, painted the triptych of The Passion *for the cathedral of Lübeck, 'the queen of the League'. His* Last Judgement *went to Dantzig. Those who commissioned portraits from him included not only middle-class Flemings such as the Moreels and Nieuwenhoves, but also Italian merchants and financiers, who at the time were to be found in every part of Europe. He painted a member of the Portinari family while Van Eyck painted an Arnolfini. On the other hand, one finds Antonello da Messina coming to Bruges to complete his training before settling in Venice.*

In fact, it was the fate of paintings of this period to come to be regarded as objects *—art objects to be ordered, bought, sold—and as a result they have become inseparably associated with commerce and patronage. The art of painting, which had formerly been reserved for the decoration of the walls of churches, was now applied to the production of pictures which could be moved from place to place, from room to room; pictures which were put on view, which provided pleasure for the art-lover and enhanced the prestige of those on whom Fortune had smiled. The Romanesque painter added life to a wall, and his fresco was like the chant of a choir of monks. Ever since, the artist has asserted his individuality, and his painting has been the work of a virtuoso.*

With the birth of the artist there came into existence the collector, who seeks out works of art to satisfy his personal taste, and sometimes in order to acquire honours which chance has failed to grant him: on the one hand a King René, on the other a financier such as Etienne Chevalier, who between them inaugurated the long line of enlightened patrons, aristocrats and commoners alike. The time was to come when this line degenerated to the point where pictures are bought purely as investments, like so many stocks and shares.

At the same time, the painter becomes concerned with matters of pure aesthetics, which demonstrate his desire to produce a work whose perfection is its own justification. He no longer paints within a larger framework, within the terms of a building, nor as an act of adoration performed within the sanctified area of a church. Instead, he strives to create something that is self-sufficient, whose worth is intrinsic, that obeys its own laws. Less consideration is paid to technical problems—the artist is quite capable of keeping in their proper place the discoveries attributed to the Van Eyck brothers and the exaggeratedly famous rules of perspective which infuse the thought and work of a Piero della Francesca, and which in future centuries were to become an obsession for anyone who took a brush in his hand. In the eighteenth century, the over-literal imitation of nature, the perfect fidelity to human anatomy, were to overshadow even the knowledge of preparing paints.

The preoccupation with aesthetics could not but affect the subjects treated—for now the painter 'treats a subject' instead of handling a theme as in the days of Romanesque art. This led to the concern with detail, the preference for the individual study of the human face, the scrupulously careful attention paid to depicting a landscape or a city as the background to the main subject, and above all the mastery of the portrait which combines technical virtuosity with a genius for observation. In their sheer faithfulness to form, painters have never bettered the fifteenth century in rendering the soul of man.

It is here, perhaps, that they most strikingly reveal their genius, and it is this that so impresses us in these painters of this Age of Transition. They faithfully record for us the faces of an age whose way of life was so different from ours, and yet whose way of thinking remains the same. Another stage is reached when the middle classes succeed in deriving a new philosophy out of classical humanism. The painter then feels more at his ease before pagan mythology than before the Nativity of the Passion, and his brush portrays the Virgin Mary in the likeness of Minerva or Venus, and God the Father as Jupiter. This development can already be foreseen in the work of Botticelli, a painter whom we know to have been torn between his art and his faith.

But he is still an exception in the group of artists assembled here, who, less than fifty years ago, were described as 'Primitives', and yet who today are considered to provide one of the most beautiful and most moving pages in the history of art. Bearing the imprint of a long tradition of religious belief which gives their works a sense of contemplation, these painters, almost without realizing what they are doing, bring the first-fruits of a world which was to see the discovery of new and unknown continents.

Régine Pernoud

Master Francke
Resurrection
Panel from the 'Englandfahrer' altar-piece
First third of the fifteenth century
Kunsthalle, Hamburg

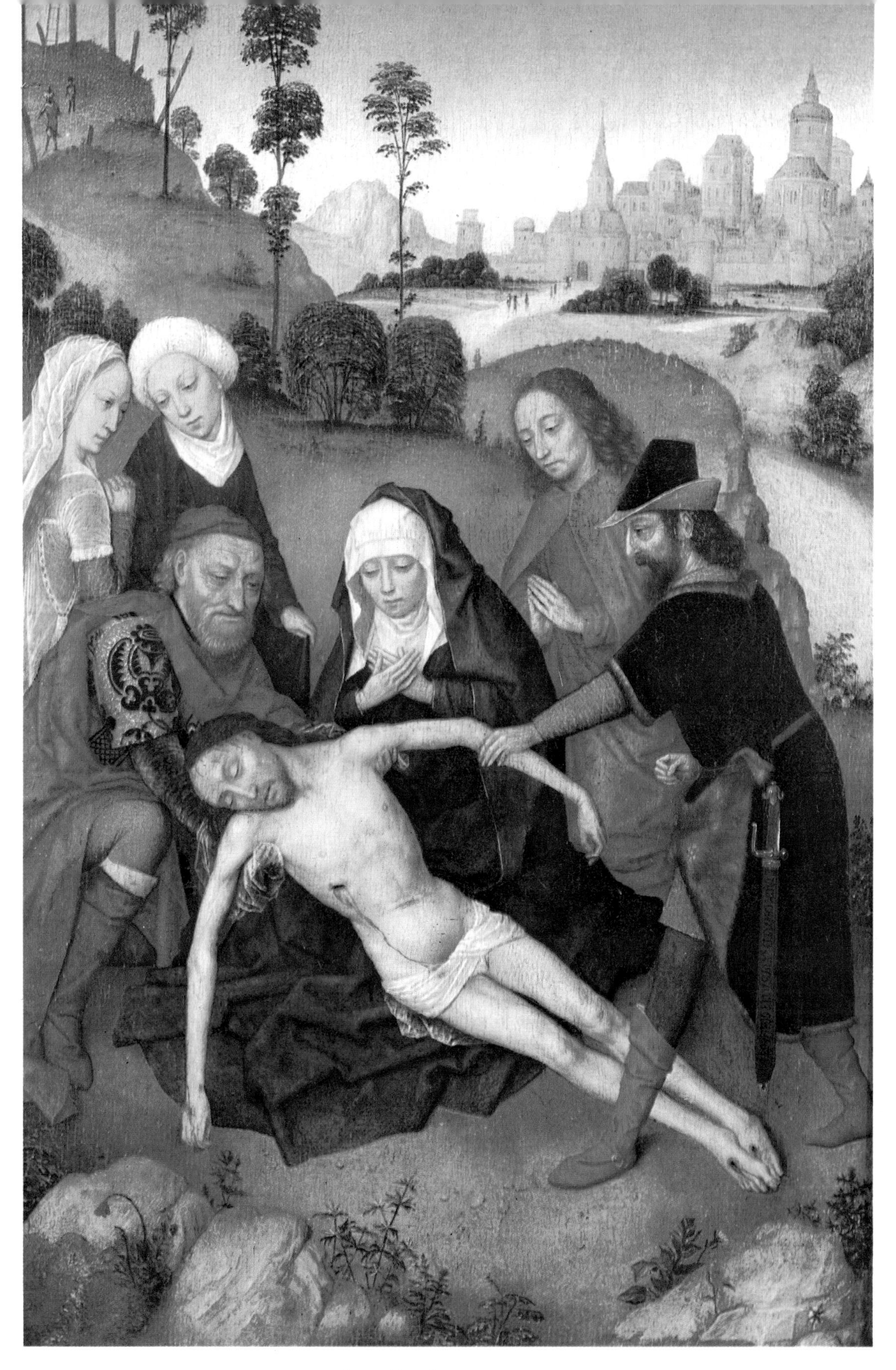

Simon Marmion
Valenciennes (1425-89)
Lamentation for the Dead Christ
Oil on wood
Lehmann Collection, New York

Jean Fouquet (*ca* 1420-*ca* 1480)
Portrait of Charles VII
Oil on wood
Louvre, Paris

Dirk Bouts
Haarlem (*ca* 1400-75)
The Justice of Emperor Otto (detail)
The Ordeal by Fire, 1475

Thouzon Altar-piece
St Andrew Chasing the Devils and *St Sebastian*
Wood panel
Ca 1410-5
Louvre, Paris

Jean Fouquet
Tours (1420-80)
Virgin and Child, 1451
Oil on wood, 36 × 32 ins.
Musée Royal des Beaux-Arts, Antwerp

Master of Moulins
Nativity with Cardinal Jean Rolin, ca 1480
Oil on wood, 21 × 28 ins.
Musée Rolin, Autun

Master of Moulins
Portrait of a Donatrix with Mary Magdalen
Ca 1490
Oil on wood, 21 × 16 ins.
Louvre, Paris

Jan Van Eyck
Madonna of Chancellor Rolin, ca 1425
Oil on wood, 26 × 24 ins.
Louvre, Paris

Nicolas Froment
Uzès-Avignon (15th century)
The Burning Bush, 1476
Oil on wood, 161 × 120 ins.
Aix-en-Provence Cathedral

Rogier Van der Weyden
Altar-piece of the Seven Sacraments, *ca* 14
Oil on wood, 79 × 38 ins.
Musée Royal des Beaux-Arts, Antwerp

Rogier Van der Weyden
Tournai 1399-Brussels 1464
Annunciation, *ca* 1464
Oil on wood, 34 × 36 ins.
Louvre, Paris

Rogier Van der Weyden
Triptych of the Braque family
Centre: *Christ the Redeemer between the Virgin and St John the Evangelist*
Louvre, Paris

Rogier Van der Weyden
Altar-piece of the Redemption
Prado, Madrid

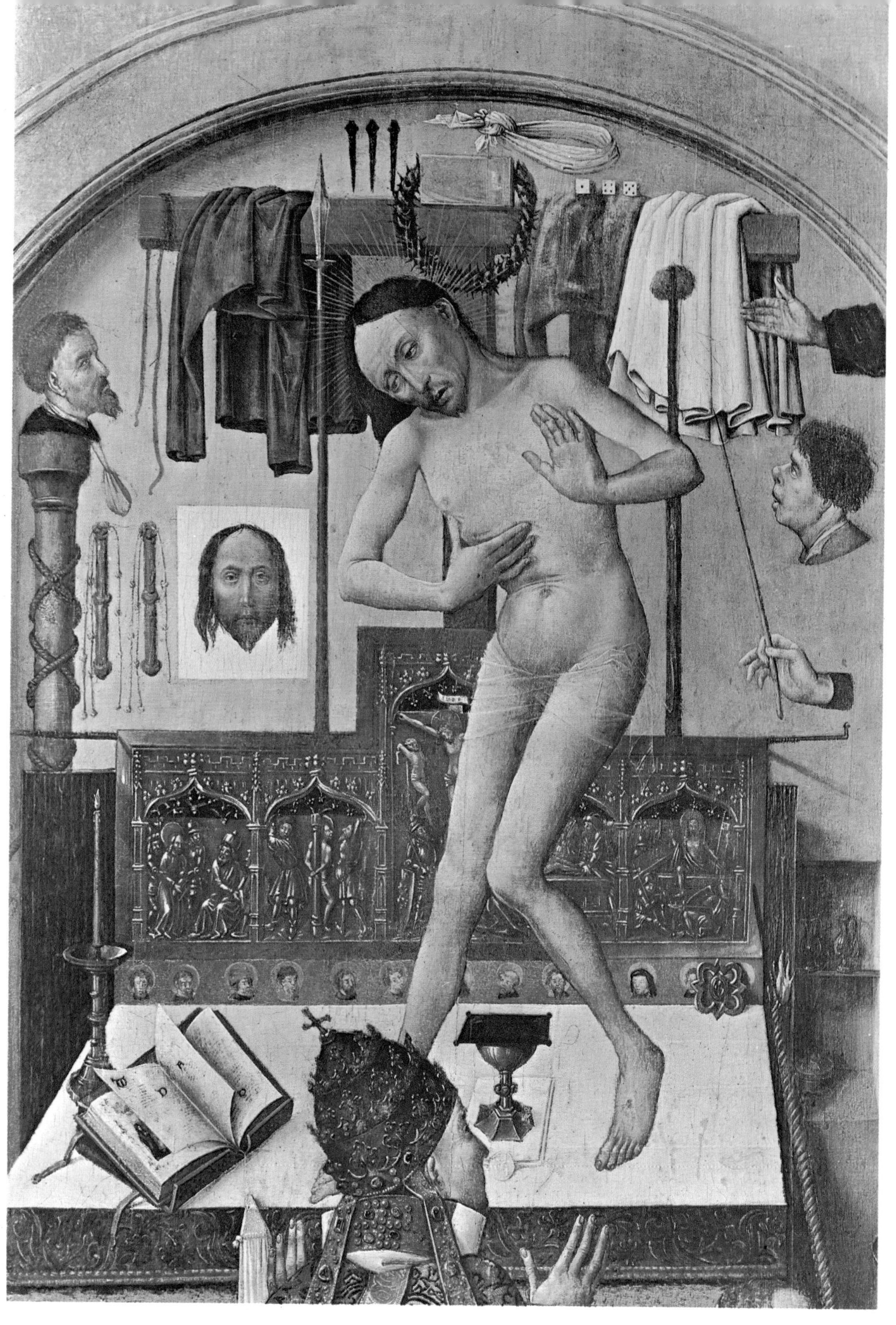

Master of Flémalle
Fifteenth century
St Gregory's Mass
Oil on wood, 33 × 29 ins.
Musée des Beaux-Arts, Brussels

Fra Angelico
Vicchio 1387-1455
The Coronation of the Virgin
Mural
Museo di San Marco, Florence

Jan Van Eyck
Madonna by the Fountain, 1439
Oil on wood, 7 × 5 ins.
Musée Royal des Beaux-Arts, Antwerp

Stephan Lochner
Madonna and Child in the Rose Garden
Oil on oak, 15th century
Wallraf-Richartz Museum, Cologne

Dirk Bouts
The Justice of Emperor Otto, ca 14
Oil on wood, 127 × 72 ins.
Musée des Beaux-Arts, Brussels

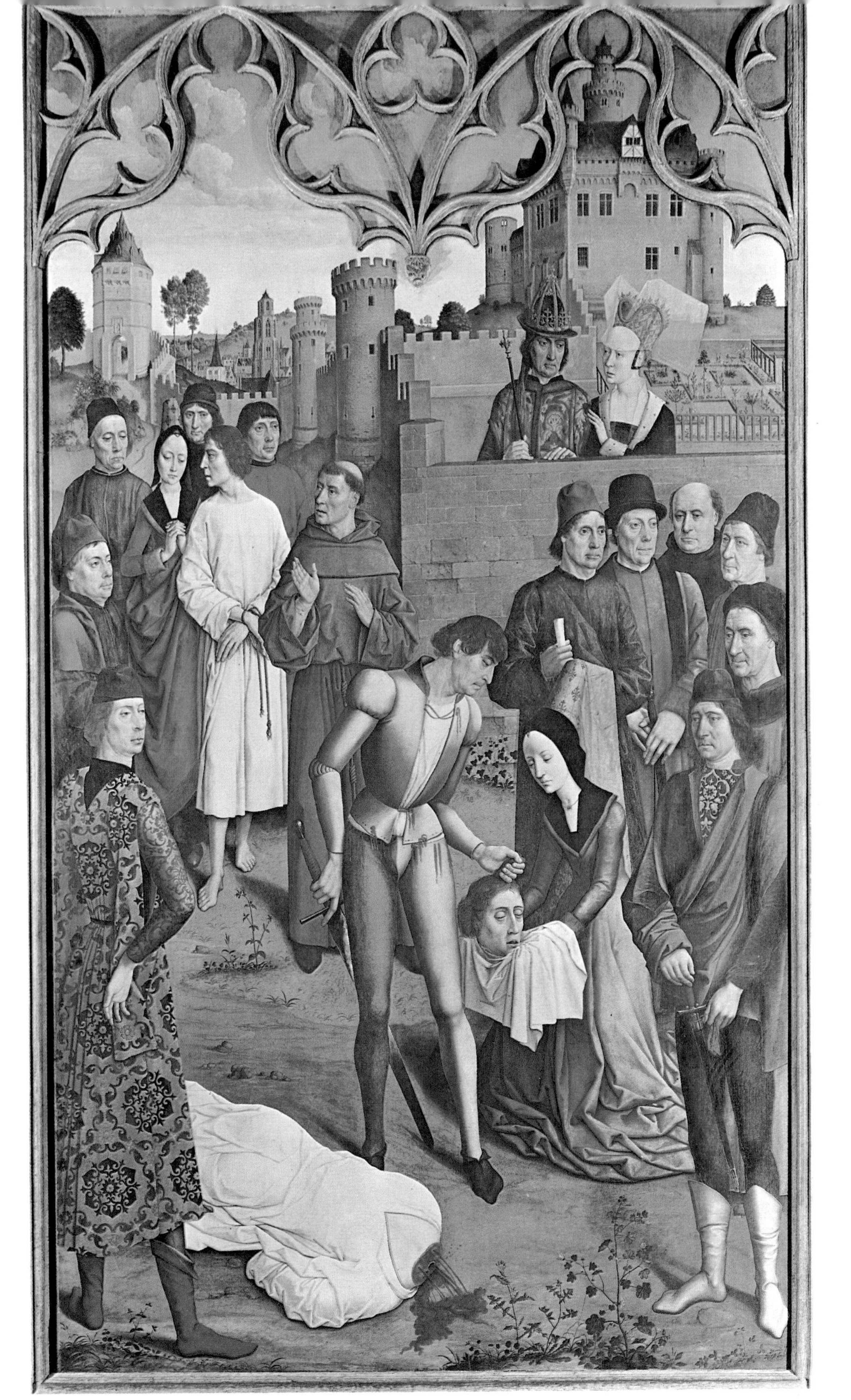

Conrad Witz
Rottweil *ca* 1410-Basle 1445
St Christopher
Kunstmuseum, Basle

Stefano di Giovanni Sassetta
Berlin 1392-*ca* 1450
The Temptation of St Antony
Oil on wood, 18 × 14 ins.
Lehmann Collection, New York

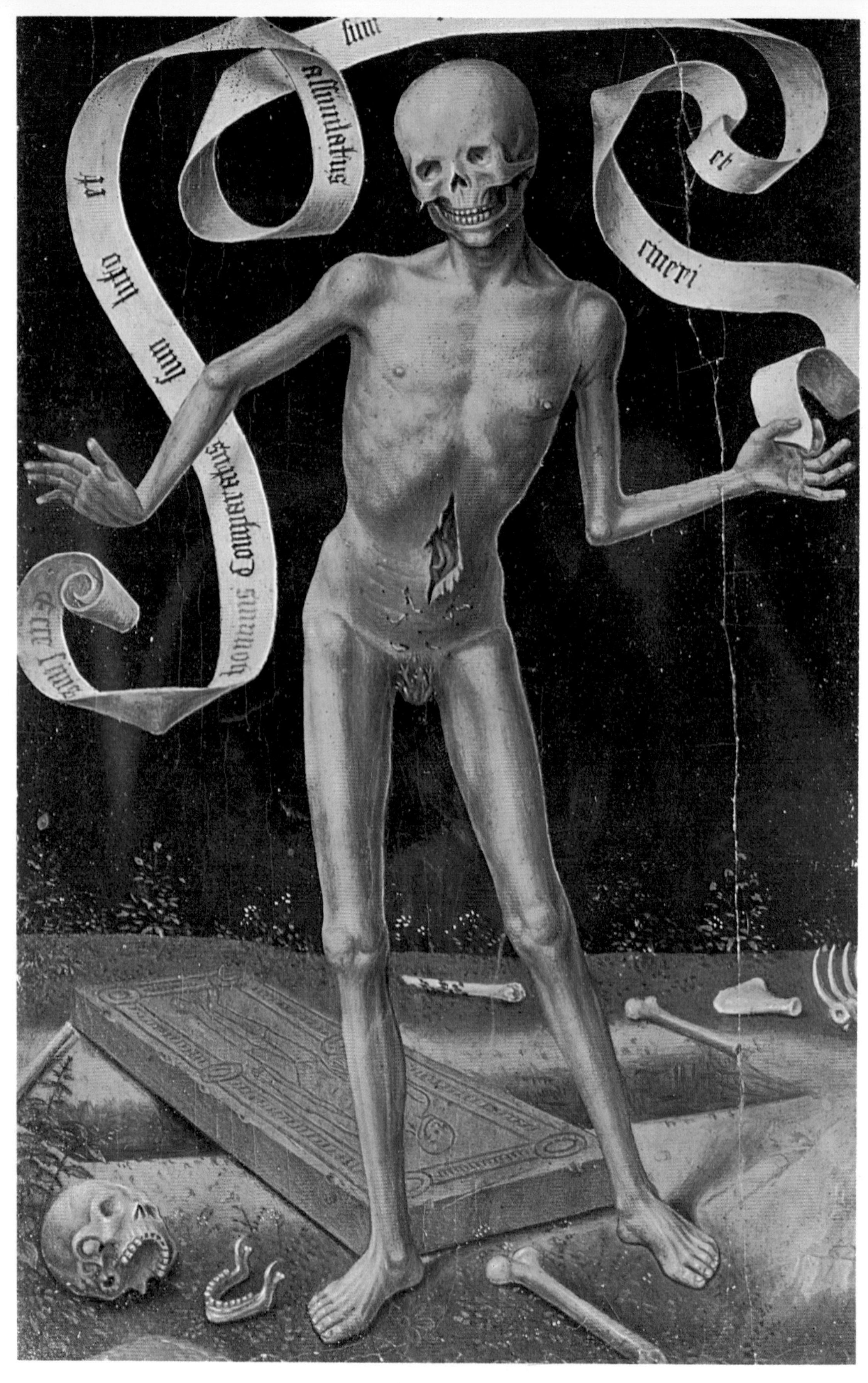

Hans Memling
Death
Musée des Beaux-Arts, Strasbourg

Hans Memling
Memlingen 1425/40-1494
The Annunciation, 1482
Oil on wood, 11 × 9 ins.
Lehmann Collection, New York

Fra Angelico
Martyrdom of Sts Cosmas and Damian, 1438-45
Oil on wood, 15 × 19 ins.
Louvre, Paris

Fra Angelico
Deposition, 1440-5
Oil on wood, 20 × 13 ins.
Museo di San Marco, Florence

Hans Memling
Vanity
Musée des Beaux-Arts, Strasbourg

Hugo Van der Goes
Virgin, Child, St Anne and Franciscan Donor
Musée d'Art Antique, Brussels

Hugo Van der Goes
Adoration of the Shepherds
Uffizi, Florence

Geertgen tot Sint Jans
Resurrection of Lazarus, *ca* 1484
Oil on wood, 50 × 38 ins.
Louvre, Paris

Hans Memling
Virgin and Child, ca 1480
Oil on wood, 26 × 18 ins.
Hôpital Saint-Jean, Bruges

Fra Angelico
Annunciation, ca 1437
Fresco
Museo di San Marco, Florence

Geertgen tot Sint Jans
Ca 1465-93
Adoration of the Magi
Oil on wood, 35 × 28 ins.
Rijksmuseum, Amsterdam

Fra Angelico
The Annunciation (The Visitation), 1430-45
Oil on wood, 76 × 76 ins.
Prado, Madrid

Fra Angelico
The Annunciation (Birth and Marriage of the Virgin),
1430-45
Oil on wood, 76 × 76 ins.
Prado, Madrid

Martin Schongauer
Ca 1445-91
Virgin and Child in an Interior
Kunstmuseum, Basle

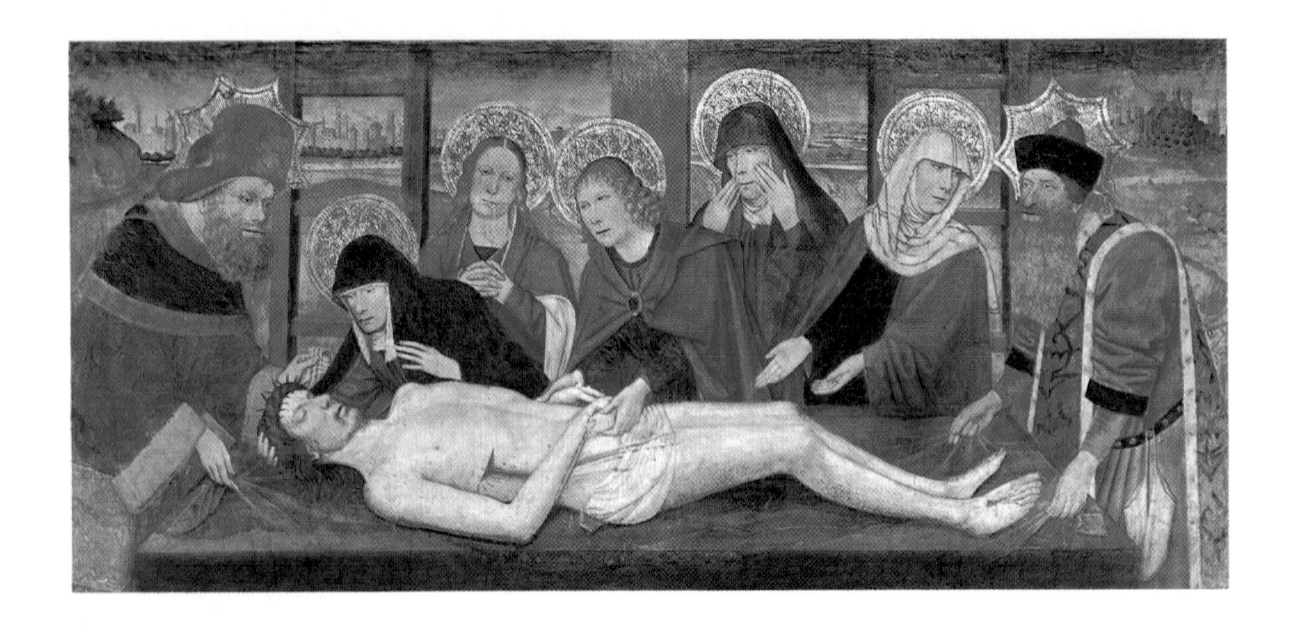

Jaime Huguet
Entombment
Louvre, Paris

Master of Flémalle
St John the Baptist and Heinrich von Werl
Prado, Madrid

Nuño Gonçalves
Ca 1438-81
St Vincent Altar-piece, ca 147(
Oil on wood
National Museum of Antique
Lis

Gerard David
Repose during the Flight into Egypt
Oil on wood, 20 × 17 ins.
Metropolitan Museum, New York

Master of the Passion of the Dominicans, Cracow
Second half of the 15th century
The Flight into Egypt
National Museum, Cracow

Nicolas Froment
The Resurrection of Lazarus, 1461
Oil on wood, 69 × 53 ins.
Uffizi, Florence

Hubert (?) Van Eyck
The Adoration of the Lamb, 1432
St Bavo's Cathedral, Ghent

Antonio Vivarini
Murano 1415-76/84
The Holy Family
Musée des Beaux-Arts, Strasbourg

Glossary of Gothic Art

Antonello da Messina (*ca* 1430-1479)

Italian painter, born in Messina, died in Venice. Son of the sculptor Giovanni degli Antoni, from whom he received his early training. After completing his apprenticeship in Rome, he went to Naples where he made the acquaintance of Zingaro. Both became great admirers of the Flemish and Dutch masters. They tried to imitate their manner, but since they were ignorant of their techniques, the results were mediocre. Antonello went to Flanders, where he showed such enthusiasm for the Flemish painters that Van Eyck accepted him as a pupil. Van Eyck not only showed a paternal affection for the young man, but also revealed to him the various techniques of painting in oils. After Van Eyck's death, Antonello returned to Italy and settled down in Venice. All the great men of the day commissioned him to paint their portraits, using the new technique. In due course, Antonello revealed the secret of oil-painting to other artists. In particular, the Bellini brothers became his close friends, and learnt Van Eyck's technique in his workshop. Antonello is considered one of the finest painters of his time. His work, particularly towards the end of his life, shows a deliberate attempt to combine Flemish and Italian art. Among his masterpieces, mention should be made of his *Saint Jerome*, strongly influenced by Van Eyck, which is in the National Gallery, and a *Portrait of a Young Patrician* in the Casa Giovanelli, Venice.

Bellini

A family of Venetian painters. Jacopo was born and worked in Venice, where he died in 1470. He had two sons, Gentile (1429-1507), who worked in Venice and Constantinople, and Giovanni (1430-1516), the most famous member of the family. Gentile's *Portrait of Mahommed II* is in the National Gallery. Giovanni's works still in Venice include the *Miracle of the Holy Cross*, the *Dead Christ*, and a *Transfiguration*.

Boccati, Giovanni (b. *ca* 1420)

Italian painter, born at Camerino. Only a few of his paintings have been identified. There is a *Virgin and Child with Angels* by him, dated 1447, in the Galerie de Pérouse; a *Virgin Surrounded by Saints* in Budapest; and *Three Archangels and the Young Tobias* in the Kaiser Friedrich Museum, Berlin. There is also a *Crucifixion* in the Lehmann Collection, New York.

Bosch, Hieronymus (*ca* 1450-1516)

Dutch painter and engraver, was born and died in 'sHertogenbosch. To a certain extent Bosch belongs to the popular tradition of mediaeval painting on account of his moralizing tendencies, his fantastic interpretation of the world, and his insight into religious problems. His detailed depiction of everyday life, on the other hand, makes him a forerunner of the realist school of the Low Countries. Bosch had a vivid imagination, which is revealed in his view of life as a continual struggle between man and his inner nature, expressed in the form of fantastic devils and other creatures, half-human and half-animal. His psychological awareness of human problems was very great. At the request of Philip II, in 1504 he painted his *Last Judgement*, now in the Musée des Beaux-Arts, Antwerp. His works are widely distributed throughout the main museums in Europe, but the Prado has a particularly fine collection.

Botticelli, Sandro (1445-1510)

Italian painter, was born and died in Florence. He was the fourth son of a local tanner, Mariano di Giovanni Filipepi. Sandro took his surname from his elder brother, who was known by his friends as *il botticello*, 'the little barrel'. At fifteen he was a pupil of Fra Filippo Lippi. The identification of his early works is a subject of dispute. It is only after 1470, the year in which he executed *Fortitude* for a series of *Virtues*, that one can date his paintings. He worked for both Lorenzo and Giuliano Medici. The famous *Primavera* dates from *ca* 1485. To his misfortune, and to ours, he came to know Savonarola, and was one of his closest supporters. He was among the painters who cast the majority of their works into the flames during the *auto-da-fé* held in Florence in 1497, and known as the 'Bonfire of Vanities'. After this date he did no more work. Poor, forgotten, suffering from religious doubts, he was only able to survive thanks to the generosity of Lorenzo the Magnificent. He died in neglect in 1510. It was not until the middle of the nineteenth century that Ruskin and the Pre-Raphaelites rendered him the praise that was his due.

Bouts, Dirk (*ca* 1415-75)

Dutch painter, born in Haarlem, where he came to know Albert Van Ouwater and Rogier Van der Weyden; it is even possible that he worked with them. None of his works of the Haarlem period is now known. In or about 1447, he went to Louvain, where he married. When his wife died he married again at the age of seventy. He was appointed official painter to the City of Louvain in 1468. He painted two historical pictures on the subject of the Emperor Otto III, for the Council-chamber of the Town Hall. In these two works he shows considerable vigour, combined with careful attention to detail and a delicate sense of composition. He is one of the first great Dutch primitives.

Breughel, Pieter (1528-69)

Flemish painter, born at Breughel in Brabant, died at Brussels. He was apprenticed to a follower of Hieronymus Bosch, who persuaded him to go and work in Antwerp for Pieter Coeck, painter to the Emperor Charles V. In 1551, Breughel set out for Italy. He was obliged to pass through France and so spent two years there. He reached Rome in 1553. It was during this period that he executed his *Naval Battle in the Straits of Messina*. Little influenced by the Italian environment, he returned to Flanders in 1554. After marrying Pieter Coeck's daughter, he settled in Brussels where he spent the rest of his life. His finest work dates from this return to Brussels. At first he devoted himself to landscapes, and then turned to religious pictures in which one finds that dramatic realism so typical of his work. Two of the paintings of this period are the *Tower of Babel*, now in Vienna, and *The Road to Calvary* in the Galleria Reale, Florence. During the last years of his life, Breughel gave up his large-scale works and painted mostly domestic scenes containing a limited number of figures. He was misunderstood by his contemporaries, who referred to him as 'Peasant Breughel' or 'Droll Breughel'.

Broederlam, Melchior

Flemish painter, born in Ypres, where he worked from 1381 to 1409. He was painter to Philip the Bold, Duke of Burgundy. In 1387, he designed the enamel panels of the Château de Hesdin. In 1395, he was working at Ghent. In 1398, on the order of Philip the Bold, he began the triptychs of the two altars at Dijon. Two panels from these triptychs, the *Annunciation* and the *Visitation*, the *Presentation in the Temple* and the *Flight into Egypt*, are now in the Musée de la Ville, Dijon. Valence Museum possesses a *Christ in the Tomb*. Some scholars assign to him a votive painting in the chapel of the Hospice at Ypres.

Brunelleschi, Filippo (1377-1446)

Italian sculptor and architect, born and died in Florence. Against the wishes of his father, a notary, he decided to devote his life to the arts. He studied in Florence and Rome, where he took an interest in architecture. Few of the sculptures of this forerunner of the Renaissance are known. A bas-relief in Florence, *Abraham's Sacrifice*, of which there is a copy in Leipzig, is attributed to him. Among his architectural works are the dome of Florence Cathedral and several buildings in Pisa, Pesaro and Milan.

Carpaccio, Vittore (*ca* 1450-*ca* 1525)

Italian painter, probably of Venetian origin. Like the Bellini brothers, he worked on the decoration of the Doge's Palace in Venice, whose large collection of historical paintings was destroyed in the fire of 1576. He also worked at the Scuola di San Girolamo in Venice, and at the Scuola di Santa Orsola, where he executed several paintings depicting scenes from the life of St Ursula, now preserved in the Accademia, Venice. His masterpiece is the *Presentation of Jesus in the Temple*, also in the Accademia. Between 1502 and 1508, he painted some ten canvases for San Giorgio degli Schiavoni. There is also an altar-piece showing St Vitalis, his wife Valeria, and other saints, which he painted in 1514 for San Vitale, as well as the *Saints Crucified*, painted in 1515 for the prior of San Antonio di Castello.

Christus, Petrus (d. *ca* 1473)

Born at Baerle, near Ghent, at an unknown date. It is known that he had settled in Bruges in 1444. In 1462, he and his wife were enrolled in the Confraternity of the Dry Tree. He worked for a long time in Bruges, where he became a member of the Guild of St Luke. In 1463, the city made a payment to him for an important commission—he had been working for the procession of the Holy Blood. He was Dean of the Painters' Guild in 1471. Thereafter there is no further reference to him, except where he is listed among the city's dead in 1473. A number of his works have survived, including the famous *Portrait of a Young Girl*, painted *ca* 1447, and now in the Kaiser Friedrich Museum, Berlin.

Coter, Colijn de

Painter who lived in Brussels during the fifteenth century. His pictures are strongly influenced by Van der Weyden. He sometimes signed his works 'Coliin de Coter pinxit me in Brabancia Brusselle'. A few paintings have been attributed to him with certainty, including the *Trinity* in the Louvre, a *Deposition from the Cross* in Messina, and *Apostles and Saints* in the Alte Pinakothek, Munich. These works place Coter in the front rank of painters.

Dalmáu, Luis

Spanish painter of the Flemish school. He was active in Barcelona between 1428 and 1460. We have no knowledge at all concerning his youth. He appears to have been appointed official painter to the king of Spain. While employed on a mission in Flanders on behalf of Alfonso V, he made a copy of the *Adoration of the Lamb* by the Van Eyck brothers, which was placed in the church of St Bavo in Ghent in 1432. In 1433, we find Dalmáu back in Barcelona, where in 1445 he completed the altar-piece of the *Virgin of the Councillors*, now in the Museo Municipal. This work, which clearly shows the influence of Van Eyck, is the only one by this artist that has survived.

David, Gerard (*ca* 1450-1523)

Painter of Dutch origin, born at Oudewater in the province of Utrecht. For three hundred years after his death his name was forgotten, and it was not until 1866 that documents referring to him were found in the archives of Bruges, the town where he worked and died. It is believed that David studied under Dirk Bouts and Albert Van Ouwater in Haarlem. From 1470 to 1480 he was in Italy: the influence of the Italian Renaissance is to be found in his works of this period. In 1483, he settled in Bruges, and became a member of the Guild of St Luke the following year. On the imprisonment of Maximilian of Austria, the new magistrates, appointed in the name of the King of France, commissioned David to paint two *Justice Scenes* for the Town Hall, which he completed in 1498. They show the influence of Florentine miniature painting. In 1501, he became Dean of the Painters' Guild. He also founded a school of miniaturists, and his wife and daughter were among his first pupils. They continued this school after the painter's death. At the beginning of the sixteenth century the main feature of David's work was his struggle against the invasion of the Italian Renaissance. Under the influence of Hans Memling and Quentin Metsys, he tried to preserve the traditions of the school of Bruges, of which he was the last great example. Adriaen Isenbrandt is said to have been one of his pupils.

Donatello (*ca* 1386-1466)

Italian sculptor, born in Florence. He had a most fertile and original genius. From the age of nineteen he was employed on the Duomo and Orsanmichele in Florence. He then worked on a series of statues in marble, including *St John the Evangelist* of Cardinal Brancacci in Sant'Angelo, Naples. He worked in Rome, and then returned to Florence, where he carved his famous *David* in the Bargello. Summoned to Padua, he executed the first great equestrian statue since antiquity, that of the Venetian condottiere Gattamelata, cast in 1447. At the age of seventy he completed one of his most beautiful works, the *Magdalen* in the Baptistery in Florence.

Dürer, Albrecht (1471-1528)

German painter and engraver, born and died in Nuremberg. He was the thirteenth of the eighteen children of Albrecht Dürer the Elder, a goldsmith of Hungarian extraction. Dürer began his apprenticeship in his father's workshop, but his interest in drawing led to his removal, *ca* 1487, to the workshop of the celebrated painter Michael Wolgemut, where he remained three years. He then set out on a journey that lasted four years. Scholars are not agreed as to what countries he visited, but it is probable that in 1492 he met the brothers of Martin Schongauer. In 1494, he was back in Nuremberg, where he married Agnes Frey. This marriage turned out unhappily. Dürer went on further travels: to Venice, in the winter of 1494-5; and again to Venice in 1505 to work with Titian and Giorgione for the Fondaco de' Mercanti. It was during this visit to Venice, which lasted till 1507, that he began his great painting, *The Feast of Rose Garlands*, now in the monastery of Strahow, near Prague. On his return to Nuremberg, he painted several important works, including *Adam and Eve* in 1507, now in the Prado; *The Massacre of the Ten Thousand Martyrs of Nicomedia* in 1508, now in the Imperial Gallery, Vienna; and the *Adoration of the Holy Trinity* in 1514, now in the Vienna Museum. From this period date many of his beautiful engravings on wood and copper. He also executed a *Prayerbook* for Maximilian I, by whom he was employed from 1512 up to the emperor's death in 1519. The great success of his engravings obliged Dürer to produce large quantities of them, leaving him little time for painting. In 1520-1, he travelled in the Low Countries, and his written notes of this journey survive. Among the paintings of his last years is the huge composition, *The Four Apostles*, now in Munich. Dürer proved himself a remarkable artist in various media, but it is above all for his copper engravings that he is best known. He was a friend of Luther and Raphael.

Erasmus, Desiderius (1469-1536)

Famous Dutch humanist, born in Rotterdam. He was educated at the very religious school at Deventer. But he very soon found himself torn between the attractions of this world and his religious aspirations, humanism and his desire for a higher perfection. Unhappy at school, he then became dissatisfied with the world, and set out on a passionate pursuit of personal fame. He quickly became the oracle of Europe, through which he travelled widely. His early writings were pious, but he soon turned to profane subjects. He then wrote his *Praise of Folly* and his celebrated *Colloquia*. He lived in a state of mental suffering, despite periods of calm, but remained all his life faithful to his own conception of himself as a humanist, as it was already being said, in his time. Towards the end of his life, his influence decreased greatly. With the help of other humanists, he founded at Louvain the Collegium Trilingue, and counted among his friends Barlaudus and Goclenius. In Holland, he was connected with the humanist Jan Everaerts, better known as the poet Johannes Secundus, famous for his Latin love-poems. Shortly before his death, the breakaway of the English Church from Rome brought him great unhappiness, for it meant the end of humanism in England, which he had long supported through such great men as Sir Thomas More.

Fouquet, Jean (*ca* 1420-*ca* 1480)

French painter and miniaturist from Tours. Illegitimate son of a priest. Fouquet was rescued from oblivion by the German collector, Georg Brentano-Laroche, who in 1805 discovered forty miniatures from the *Heures d'Etienne Chevalier*. Contemporary sources throw little light on his work. A few of the miniatures from the *Jewish Antiquities* in the Bibliothèque Nationale, Paris, have been identified as being in his hand. In his work one finds the monumental breadth of a Dirk Bouts or a Piero della Francesca, who were his contemporaries. Fouquet travelled in Italy and came under Italian influences, particularly as regards his ornamentation and use of perspective. On his return, Fouquet worked both as a portrait-painter—see his *Portrait of Charles VII* in the Louvre—and illuminator, first under Charles VII and then under Louis XI. As a painter, one of his masterpieces is his *Virgin and Child* in the Musée des Beaux-Arts, Antwerp. Jean Fouquet is often considered one of the founders of French art.

Fra Angelico (1387-1455)

Dominican father and painter, whose real name was Giovanni da Fiesole, born in Vicchio in Tuscany. He is considered one of the greatest Florentine artists of the Quattrocento, on account of his gracefulness, the freshness of his colours, and the profound religious inspiration of his paintings. He decorated the Convent of San Marco in Florence, which contained the *Annunciation*, the *Coronation of the Virgin*, the *Deposition*, etc., as well as all the cells. In each of these the painter recorded a holy scene, a text for meditation and prayer, a scene from the New Testament. He also decorated the Chapel of St Stephen and St Lawrence in the Vatican.

Froment, Nicolas

French painter of the fifteenth century, born at Uzès, died at Avignon. Froment is one of the most important representatives of the French primitives. During their day, these painters were despised by the public, who were much more interested in Italian art. With Enguerrand Charonton, Nicolas Froment introduced the new Flemish style to the Court of the Popes at Avignon. In about 1450, after the popes had left Avignon, these two artists gathered together a large number of pupils, who formed the realist stream of the Provençal primitive school. One also comes across this realist style—considered 'crude' at the time—in the Avignon *Pietà* and the *Resurrection of Lazarus*. Froment pushed his realism a long way, not hesitating to use an actual corpse as a model. In his work the dominating features of French art make their appearance—balance, realism, and a soberly expressed concern with the problems of human existence.

Geertgen tot Sint Jans (*ca* 1465-*ca* 1493)

One of the great Dutch painters of the end of the fifteenth century. He worked in the studio of Albert Van Ouwater. He painted a triptych for the main altar of the Chapel of the Knights of St John in Haarlem, depicting the *Calvary*, *Deposition*, and *Resurrection*. One of the panels is in the Kunsthistorisches Museum, Vienna. His other works include *Christ in Agony* in Utrecht, *The Resurrection of Lazarus* in the Louvre, and a fine series of pictures in the Rijksmuseum, Amsterdam.

Ghiberti, Lorenzo (1370-1455)

Italian painter and sculptor, born and died in Florence. In 1403, he began work on the famous door of the Baptistery, which many scholars regard as marking the beginning of Renaissance sculpture. This door, divided into twenty-eight reliefs, took twenty years to complete. Vasari, 'a poor critic, but a man who saw with the eyes of the Renaissance' (Carlo Steiner), did not hesitate to accuse Ghiberti of ingenuousness: 'The draperies still retain something of the old manner of Giotto,' he wrote. Michelangelo, on the other hand, pronounced the two doors that Ghiberti designed to be worthy to be the gates of Paradise.

Ghirlandaio, Domenico (1449-94)

Italian painter, born and died in Florence. He soon earned fame and became one of the most sought-after artists, receiving numerous commissions. He took his inspiration from Veneziano, Verrocchio, and Don Diaminte. He lacked the lightness of touch and the airy colours of these masters. His style is more incisive, heavier perhaps, but the strength of his drawing and the expressiveness of his characters make him one of the most significant painters of the Quattrocento. Ghirlandaio was also influenced by the Flemish masters, and there is no doubt that he was particularly familiar with the work of Hugo Van der Goes. The *Portrait of an Old Man and his Grandson* in the Louvre is a typical example of Ghirlandaio's style. He decorated the Sassetti Chapel in Florence, as well as Santa Maria Novella, which contains his *Birth of the Virgin*.

Giotto, Ambrogio Bondone (1266-1336)

Giotto was born in Colle di Vespighano, the son of a peasant, and was himself a shepherd. As a painter he was a visionary, who made man once again part of the divine creation, and reintroduced the taste for truth learnt from nature herself. Once and for all, he rid painting of Byzantine influence. His trees, flowers, and animals, which had merely a symbolic value to men of the early Middle Ages, take on a reality of their own. In the words of Carlo Steiner, 'the new men, the poets of the *dolce stil novo*, discover ways of expressing a completely reawakened world by considering the life of a flower opening its petals in the morning, the dew sparkling on the branch in the evening, the tranquillity of dusk which stirs thoughts of regret in man's heart. In Umbria, Jacopone da Todi was writing the *Stabat Mater* at a time that only slightly antedates Giotto. How can one relate this lyrical poem, which is so profoundly human and seems to spring from the very soul of the people, this tragedy of the Wife and the Mother, to the Queen of the great *maestàs*, mystical through the sheer power of withdrawal? Seen in this light, Giotto, the former shepherd, no longer appears an inexplicable prodigy, but as one of the links in the chain, one of the basic features of one of the most perfect civilizations that man has ever known.' As a fresco-painter, Giotto showed himself to be remarkably accomplished. He passed on his knowledge and experience to his pupils, who in turn handed them on to the whole world. Dante considered him 'the greatest painter of mankind'. Leonardo da Vinci thought that he and Masaccio were the only ones who had remained faithful to truth. Vasari regarded him as 'the ancestor of painting'. Degas wrote in one of his notebooks, 'O Giotto, let me see Paris'. Giotto decorated the Upper Church at Assisi and the Arena Chapel, Padua. There is a magnificent *Madonna* by him in Florence.

Goes, Hugo Van der (*ca* 1440-82)

Famous Flemish painter, born in Ghent, one of the greatest painters of his time. He became a member of the Painters' Guild in Ghent in 1465. It has been suggested that the resemblances between the work of Van der Goes and that of the Van Eyck brothers is not due to the former having been a pupil of the latter, but to Van der Goes' careful and attentive study of the Van Eycks. In 1467, Van der Goes was summoned to Bruges to carry out work in honour of the occasion of the marriage of Charles the Bold and Margaret of York. His fame spread rapidly, and an agent of the Medicis commissioned from him a triptych for Santa Maria

Novella in Florence. The central panel shows the *Adoration of the Shepherds*, while on the wings are to be seen the agent himself, Tommaso Portinari, and his family. In 1472, he painted his *St John in the Desert*, now in the Alte Pinakothek, Munich, which, from the point of view of the landscape, can be compared with the *Adoration of the Lamb* in Ghent. At the age of forty-six, Van der Goes entered the monastery of the Roode Clooster at Soignies as a lay-brother. He was still able to work. Important people came and visited him, including Maximilian himself, the son-in-law of Charles the Bold. On his return from a journey undertaken in the company of his brother, who was also a monk, he was overcome by a fit of madness, and tried to commit suicide. At the Roode Clooster he was looked after with the greatest care and attention, and made a partial recovery. But he died a few months later. This first-class painter was also a great miniaturist.

Gonçalves, Nuño (*ca* 1438-*ca* 1481)

Portuguese painter. He worked at the court of King Alfonso of Portugal, and painted the *Polyptych of St Vincent* in Lisbon Cathedral. For the Convent of the Trinity in Lisbon he painted a *Christ at the Pillar.* Gonçalves was a painter who was technically perfect, but he sometimes reveals the influence of the Italian school.

Grünewald, Mathias (*ca* 1466-1528)

German painter and engraver, born in Würzburg. Best known for his Isenheim altar-piece, now in the Colmar museum. The painter Joachim von Sandrart (1606-88), wrote, 'Mathias Grünewald, alias Mathias of Aschaffenburg, is one of the best of the German primitive painters. In the art of pencil and brush he yields to no one; on the contrary, he is in fact the equal of the finest and most famous artists. It is to be regretted that this exceptionable person should have been forgotten, and that I have been unable to find anyone who could give me any information about him.' This is a particularly valuable statement, in view of the fact that in the fifteenth century painters in general treated their colleagues with complete indifference. Grünewald was acquainted with Dürer. During his stay in Strasbourg, Grünewald painted his beautiful portrait of Philip II of Hanau Lichtenberg and Anne Isenburg. Although Grünewald is in a sense a forerunner, from many points of view he can still be said to retain certain Gothic ideas. He was a profoundly original artist with a very sound knowledge of his craft. He introduced into painting the universality of Christ's message.

Holbein the Elder, Hans (*ca* 1460-1524)

Famous German painter, born at Augsburg. With Cranach, he preserved the old traditions of German painting. It is believed that Holbein the Elder worked in Martin Schongauer's shop in Colmar, and that he was indirectly influenced by Rogier Van der Weyden. In 1499, he became a citizen of Ulm. From this period date the *Death of the Virgin*, now in Basle Museum, *Thirteen Scenes of the Passion*, the tryptych in the Augsburg Museum, and the *Madonna and Child* in Nuremberg. He was extremely productive, and maintained a high standard in his work, as can be seen in the sixteen fine scenes from the *Life of the Virgin* in Munich. He was also an excellent draughtsman.

Holbein the Younger, Hans (1497-1543)

German painter and engraver, son of Hans

Holbein the Elder, born at Augsburg, died in London. Together with his brother Ambrosius he worked in his father's shop until 1514. The first known work by Holbein the Younger is the *Virgin and Child* in the Basle Museum. It is probable that Holbein left Basle for Antwerp, whence, provided with letters of introduction to various important people, including Sir Thomas More, he took ship for England. Among these letters was one from Erasmus, who was one of Holbein's friends. From this period date his portraits of *Archbishop Warham* (1527) and *Sir Henry Guildford*, now in Windsor Castle, *Thomas Godsalve and his Son*, and *Sir Bryan Tuke*. Having achieved fame, he painted portraits of *Henry VIII*, *Ann of Cleves*, *Jane Seymour*, and *Thomas Howard, Duke of Norfolk*. He died of the plague in London in 1543, at the age of forty-six.

Huguet, Jaime (*ca* 1414-92)

Spanish painter active in Barcelona during the fifteenth century. He worked in various monasteries in and around Barcelona.

Leyden, Lucas Van (1494-1538)

Dutch painter and engraver, born and died in Leyden. Van Mander states that he learnt to paint on glass at the age of nine; at ten he was an engraver, and at twelve he was using an egg base for his painting of the *History of St Hubert* for Van Lockhorst. He was acquainted with Dürer and Jan Mabuse. Only a very few of his paintings have been authenticated, but these include two remarkable works, a *Last Judgement* in Leyden Museum and *Lot and his Daughters* in the Louvre.

Limbourg Brothers

Illuminators from Limbourg, active at the beginning of the fifteenth century. They were among the greatest miniaturists of their day. There were three brothers—Pol, who died after 1416; Hennequin, who died before 1439; and Hermann, who also died before 1439. From 1402 onwards, the first two were in Dijon in the service of Philip the Bold, Duke of Burgundy, and after his death in 1404, they continued in the service of John the Fearless. The *Breviary of John the Fearless*, now in the British Museum, was probably the work of Pol. After 1405, the three brothers became attached to the court of John of France, Duke of Berry. The *Belles Heures*, called the *Heures d'Ailly*, now in the Rothschild Collection in Paris, were executed between 1406 and 1414 for the Duke of Berry. Their workshop was particularly productive during this period. Their masterpiece, the *Très Riches Heures du Duc de Berry*, now in the Musée Condé, Chantilly, dates from about 1415, and was completed by Jean Colombe of Bourges between 1435 and 1439. The miniatures by the Limbourg brothers consist of thirty-nine large compositions and twenty-four small ones, depicting scenes from the Old and New Testaments, and the famous *Calendar*. Although they were born in Holland, the style and colours employed by the Limbourg brothers belong to the art of the French miniaturists of the beginning of the fifteenth century.

Lippi, Fra Filippo (*ca* 1406-69)

Florentine painter and monk. He abandoned the monastery to devote himself to painting. For a time he led an adventurous life. Vasari even states that he was seized by some Barbary pirates who were sailing past Ancona, and was kept in captivity for eighteen months. At first he was influenced by Masaccio and Masolino, but he managed to free himself of them, and indeed his work lacks their austerity. 'It was given to two painters,' wrote Jean Dupuy, 'to show how the traditional painting of Giotto could accord with science. They were both monks—one, Fra Angelico, an exemplary Dominican, the other Fra Filippo, a Carmelite of little virtue. The madonnas of Fra Angelico appear as sexless beings, all in gold and azure blue; those of Filippo Lippi seem to be delighted at finding themselves on earth.' Fra Filippo is a great artist, and in some ways a forerunner of Botticelli (see, for example, *The Dance of Salome*). He mingled Quattrocento realism with what remained of the purest mediaeval mysticism. He was buried in Spoleto Cathedral, where Lorenzo Medici had a splendid tomb made for him.

Lochner, Stephan (d. 1451)

German painter, born in Meersburg, died in Cologne. One of the most important representatives of the Cologne school which developed towards the end of the fourteenth century. Like Fra Angelico in Italy, Lochner displays a mystical gracefulness in his paintings which reflects a tranquillity achieved through religion. He has a very subtle technique. His masterpiece is the *Dombild*, a triptych in Cologne Cathedral, but his *Madonna and Child in the Rose Garden*, in the Wallraf-Richartz Museum, Cologne, is considered not only his most beautiful but also his earliest work. Other works by this painter, who has been described as 'the last of the Gothic artists', are to be found in museums in Cologne, Berlin, Bonn, Darmstadt, Frankfurt, Munich and London.

Marmion, Simon (1425-89)

Painter and illuminator, born and died at Valenciennes. He became official painter to the Duke of Burgundy. He was active in Tournai, Valenciennes, and Amiens. His *Jesus Meditating on the Passion* and *Portrait of a Young Man* are in Aix Museum; the *Scenes from the Life of St Bertin* in the Kaiser Friedrich Museum, Berlin; and the *Coronation of Frederick III by Pope Nicholas V* in Nuremberg.

Martini, Simone (1284-1344)

Italian painter, born in Siena, died in Avignon. In 1315, he painted the *Maestà* in the Town Hall, Siena. He travelled, and in 1320 he is reported at Naples, where he was given several commissions. At Pisa, he painted and signed the polyptych in Santa Catarina. In 1328, he was again at work in the Town Hall in Siena, where he painted opposite the *Maestà*, an equestrian portrait of *The Condottiere Guido da Fogliano*, remarkable for its strict limitation to bare essentials. In 1333, he painted the beautiful *Annunciation* in the Uffizi. Finally, in 1339 he was summoned to Avignon by Pope Benedict XII, where he arrived with his wife and brother, Donato. He worked at Notre-Dame-des-Doms. He met Petrarch, and it is said that he painted a portrait of Laura. He died in Avignon in 1344. Simone Martini holds a very important position in the history of painting of the Trecento on account of the nobility of his compositions, the elegance of his draughtsmanship, and the subtlety in his use of colour. A large number of his works have survived.

Masaccio (1401-28)

Italian painter, born in 1401, died in Rome. His real name was Tommaso di Ser Giovanni di Mone. He was a most precocious artist, who possibly came under the influence of Donatello and Brunelleschi. He worked in Florence, where he painted frescoes in the Brancacci Chapel, and later in Rome. A number of his other paintings have survived, including portraits of men and women, in particular his *Portrait of an Unknown Old Man*, painted on a large brick, and now in the Uffizi. Vasari deplored the fact that Masaccio was so little esteemed during his lifetime. He was buried in the Carmelite monastery in Florence, but no inscription was engraved on his tomb. This great artist, who died at the age of twenty-seven, had a strong influence on the Quattrocento.

Master of Flémalle

Flemish painter of the fifteenth century. For a long time he was identified with Robert Campin, who died in 1444. The Master of Flémalle probably worked in Bruges, Liège, Tournai, and Northern France. With Van Eyck, he can be considered the founder of the Flemish School.

Master of Moulins

French painter, who was active in the old French province of Le Bourbonnais between 1480 and 1500. Little is known about the existence of this great artist. He was sometimes identified with Jean Perréal, a painter famous in his day whose work has mysteriously disappeared. This theory has now been abandoned. The following is a brief list, in chronological order, of some of the authentic works of the Master of Moulins: the *Nativity*, *ca* 1480, in Autun Museum; the *Portrait of Cardinal Charles II of Bourbon at Prayer*, in the Alte Pinakothek, Munich; the *Child Adored by Angels*, *ca* 1490, in the Brussels Museum; and the famous triptych in Moulins Cathedral, *ca* 1498-1500.

Melozzo da Forlì (1438-94)

Italian painter, born and died in Forlì. Little is known about his life. He was probably acquainted with Piero della Francesca in Arezzo, and may have stayed a while in Urbino. From 1476 to 1490 he worked in Rome. There is a fresco by him in the Galleria Vaticana, the *Nomination of Platina as Prefect of the Vatican*, and he executed the paintings which ornament the arches of the chapel of the Tesorio in Loreto.

Memling, Hans (*ca* 1435-1494)

Flemish painter of German origin, born at Memlingen near Mainz. He worked in Bruges. Little is known about his life. The Bruges archives show that he became a citizen of the town, that he married, and had three children. It is thought that he was a pupil of Rogier Van der Weyden. Memling revived the Bruges school, which had been passing through a period of decline. The Hôpital Saint-Jean in Bruges contains some of his finest works, including the *Shrine of St Ursula*, which shows scenes of the saint's life on small panels; the *Adoration of the Magi*, in which according to tradition, the painter himself is depicted in the guise of the donor, a figure in black who is contemplating the scene; and the famous diptych of the *Virgin with Apple*, the gift of Martin Van Nieuwenhoven, mayor of Bruges and governor of the Hôpital Saint-Jean. 'This is,' wrote Huysman, 'perhaps the most beautiful madonna that Memling ever painted. One cannot analyse her features. One can only say that she has blond hair, large lowered eyes, a long straight nose, and a small mouth, an adorable mouth which is like a crumpled flower with the slight crinkles you find after a mild frost. And to tell the truth, I really do not know whether she is made of flesh and bones, for her skin is as white as the pith of an elder-tree, and her body is as frail as the stalk of a flower.' The Hôpital Saint-Jean also contains two masterpieces, the *Mystical Marriage of St Catherine* and the *Portrait of Marie, Daughter of Guillaume Moreel*, or the *Sybil Zambetha*.

Michelangelo (1475-1564)

Painter, sculptor, architect, engineer, and poet. Born in Caprese, near Florence, died in Rome. Worked for Lorenzo Medici and Pope Julius II. One of the greatest artists of all time.

Piero della Francesca (*ca* 1410-92)

Tuscan painter, born in Borgo San Sepolcro, a small town in the Tiber valley. Worked in Florence under Domenico Veneziano. His earliest known work, the *Baptism of Christ*, is in the National Gallery. In 1440, he was at the court of the Duke of Urbino, one of the most important centres of the 'early' Italian Renaissance. He then worked in Rome for Pope Pius II. Roberto Longhi published a monograph on Piero della Francesca in 1927, while André Suarès devoted a chapter to him in his *Condottiere*. In the words of Carlo Steiner, André Malraux 'considers his rediscovery one of the most important events marking the change between our way of seeing and that of our predecessors'. Piero della Francesca influenced Tuscan, Umbrian and Venetian painting. Among his pupils were Signorelli and Perugino. Mantegna, Bellini, Giorgione, and Carpaccio were all indebted to him. He spent his later life at the court of the Montefeltros, in Urbino and Arezzo. His frescoes are examples of Quattrocento art at its greatest. His masterpiece is the *History of the Holy Cross* in Arezzo, painted between 1452 and 1460.

Raphael (1483-1520)

Painter, sculptor and architect, born in Urbino. In 1499, he went to work in the shop of Perugino. In 1504, he went to Florence and discovered the new painting of Leonardo da Vinci and Michelangelo. Thereafter his manner changed completely. His friendship with Fra Bartolommeo was also decisive, and had a profound influence on his style. It was at about this time that he painted the small *St George* in the Louvre. Pope Julius II's architect, Bramante, who was also from Urbino, succeeded in getting Raphael commissioned to decorate the Vatican, and from 1509 to 1513 he was the pope's favourite painter. Every nobleman and important dignitary wished to possess a work by Raphael, whose output became very large. Broken health and overwork brought on a fever, from which he died on 7 April 1520.

Rosselli, Cosimo di Lorenzo (1439-1507)

Italian painter who specialized in historical works, born and died in Florence. He was a pupil of Benozzo Gozzoli. He may have painted the fresco of *The Blessed Philip Benizi Receiving the Habit of the Servites from the Virgin Mary* in Sant'Annunciazione in Florence. In 1480, he was in Rome, whither he had been summoned by Sixtus IV in order to decorate the Sistine Chapel, along with Signorelli, Ghirlandaio and Perugino. Rosselli painted *The Crossing of the Red Sea*, *Moses Receiving the Tables of the Law*, *The Sermon on the Mount*, and *The Last Supper*. He later worked at Lucca, where he painted the tympanum of a doorway of San Martino.

Sassetta, Stefano di Giovanni (1392-1451)

Italian painter in the tradition of Simone Martini. He had great gifts of originality and imagination, which however were always tempered by that mystical freshness so dear to the Sienese painters. Among his most striking works are his *Journey of the Magi* and *The Temptation of St Antony*.

Schongauer, Martin (*ca* 1445-91)

Painter and engraver of the Alsatian school. He worked in Colmar for most of his life. His father, a jeweller from Augsburg, settled in Colmar *ca* 1440. He was both a great engraver and great painter. T. de Wyzéwa has written of his *Virgin in the Rose Garden*, 'This is one of those almost impersonal works whose attraction is felt through the senses rather than the mind and which force the most ardent art critic to give up discussing parallels and theories for a moment and enjoy sheer beauty in silence'. After Schongauer's death, Dürer went to see his three brothers, and this visit has been interpreted as an act of homage to the dead painter.

Signorelli, Luca (1441-1523)

Italian painter, born and died at Cortona. He painted some famous frescoes depicting *Antichrist*, *Hell*, *The Resurrection*, and *Paradise* in Orvieto Cathedral. These are powerful works which reveal a remarkable technique and knowledge of anatomy. He also painted frescoes in Cortona Cathedral (1502), and then went to Rome to assist in the decoration of the Vatican for Julius II. He worked with Pollaiuolo. Michelangelo came under his influence.

Titian (Tiziano Vecelli) (1477-1576)

Italian painter and engraver. His family belonged to the gentry. His exceptional gifts were discovered at an early age. He was first a pupil of Sebastiano Zuccato, and then of the Bellini brothers. From 1507 onwards he worked under Giorgione. In 1511, after Giorgione's death, he painted three frescoes for the Scuola del Santo, Padua. Then he went to work at the court of Alfonso d'Este, Duke of Ferrara. In about 1523, he painted his *Bacchus and Ariadne*, now in the National Gallery. Thereafter, success followed success, and 'princes and kings contended for his works'. He painted portraits of Charles V, Pope Paul III, and Philip II of Spain. He was a friend of Vasari, and consorted with Michelangelo and Aretino. His output was enormous. From this period dates *The Man with the Glove* in the Louvre. Titian lived a pleasant life, and was laden with honours. After the death of his wife he withdrew to the outskirts of Venice where he divided his time between his work and the education of his four children. He died of the plague on 27 August 1576, and was buried in the church of the Frari, for which he had painted a huge *Assumption* which is now in the Accademia, Venice.

Uccello, Paolo (1397-1475)

Italian painter, born and died in Florence. The name Uccello was given to him on account of his love of birds. In his youth he was a jeweller and a pupil of Lorenzo Ghiberti, who probably taught him to paint. From Manetti he learnt geometry, a subject in which he excelled, and which led him to declare that it was perspective that gave a painting its charm. Indeed, Vasari wrote a century later, 'Paolo Uccello would have been the most ingenious painter since Giotto, if only he had spent on his figures of men and animals the hours that he wasted in studies of perspective'. To-day, that statement appears somewhat severe. Uccello sacrificed a great deal to his love of perspective, and we are grateful to him for this. The formulation of the rules of perspective were to revolutionize painting. It required all the genius of this great artist of the Quattrocento to combine the spirituality inherited from the Sienese with mathematical theory. Up to this time, space had been rather poorly assimilated, and many painters had not even felt the need to use perspective to reproduce disappearance in the distance, since this had become confused with contemplation. One can easily understand Uccello's enthusiasm, which sometimes led to repetitiousness, on overcoming the third dimension.

Van der Weyden, Goswyn (b. *ca* 1465, d. after 1538)

Flemish painter, born in Brussels, son of Peter Van der Weyden. He settled in Antwerp. He became a member of the Painters' Guild in 1503, and was dean in 1514 and again in 1530. The *Coronation of the Virgin*, which he painted for the abbey of Tongerloo, dates from 1535. Among his best known works are a *Virgin and Child* in the Kaiser Friedrich Museum, Berlin, and a *Christ on the Cross* in the Musée Marmottan, Paris.

Van der Weyden, Rogier (*ca* 1399-1464)

Flemish painter, born in Tournai, died in Brussels. He is also called Rogier de la Pasture. There has been a great deal of speculation about his work and even his life. 'What we know about him,' wrote Erik Larsen, 'is slight. There is no documentary evidence available to identify with certainty any of the works habitually attributed to him. He never signed a picture, and the few contemporary records which have so far been discovered merely serve to complicate an already confused situation...' Only a system of cross-checking references can throw any light on the life of this great artist, and his works can be authenticated only on stylistic grounds. Together with Jacques Daret, Van der Weyden became a pupil of Robert Campin early in life. This was during the time that Hubert and Jan Van Eyck were painting their masterpieces. According to the records of the Painters' Guild in Tournai the young Rogier became apprenticed to Robert Campin on 5 March 1427, and on 1 August 1432—the year in which the Van Eyck brothers completed the *Adoration of the Lamb*—he became a member of the Tournai Guild. On the other hand, other documents indicate that from 1425 he was living in Brussels, where he married and had a son. It has even been suggested that there were two Van der Weyden brothers, the elder living in Brussels and the younger in Bruges. This shows the confusion in our knowledge of the painter's life. When Nicolas Rollin, chancellor to Philip the Good, Duke of Burgundy, founded the celebrated Hospice in Beaune in 1443, Rogier Van der Weyden was commissioned to decorate the chapel, where he painted *The Last Judgement*. This is one of the largest compositions in Gothic art, after the altar-piece of the *Adoration of the Lamb*. Van der Weyden's works are to be found in museums throughout Europe and the United States: *Christ the Redeemer between the Virgin and St John* is in the Louvre; *The Adoration of the Magi* is in the Alte Pinakothek, Munich; the *Portrait of Francesco d'Este* in the Metropolitan Museum, New York; the *Descent from the Cross* in the Prado, Madrid, etc. Rogier Van der Weyden introduced into Gothic art a sense of movement, pathos, and, in his portraits of women, a certain sensuality. He is in the front rank of Flemish painters, and had an influence on Memling, Bouts, Van der Goes and Gerard David, as well as on foreign schools, particularly in Germany and Poland.

Van Eyck, Hubert (*ca* 1366-1426)

Jan Van Eyck's elder brother, born at Eyck-sur-Meuse, died in Ghent. There are references to Hubert having had his own workshop. In 1413, for example, a certain Jan van Visch bequeathed to his daughter a painting 'from Master Hubert's workshop', but the records are vague. We know only that Hubert worked with his brother on the St Bavo altar-piece, and that he added his name to Jan's in a quatrain. The identification of any further works by him is at present highly speculative.

Van Eyck, Jan (*ca* 1385-1441)

Born at Eyck-sur-Meuse, died in Bruges on 8 July 1441. Our knowledge of the life of Jan Van Eyck comes mainly from the accounts discovered among the public records of Lille, and published by the great mediaevalist, Comte de Laborde. In 1422, Jan was working on the decorations, now destroyed, of the Palace of The Hague. In 1425, he was appointed Court Painter and valet to Philip the Good, Duke of Burgundy. He was active in Lille from 1425 to 1427, still in the service of Philip the Good, for whom he worked up to his death. He often travelled abroad, sometimes on secret missions. In 1428, he was attached to a diplomatic mission which visited Lisbon in order to arrange the marriage between Philip and Isabella, daughter of King John II of Portugal. On his return he settled in Bruges where he bought a house with 'the fourth part of his earnings as a painter', *ca* 1431. According to Van Mander, *ca* 1410 Jan 'invented oil-painting'. A third brother, Lambert, is mentioned as having been in the service of the Duke of Burgundy, but it is not known whether he had a workshop and produced any paintings. As to 'Margaret, a painter and sister of the Van Eyck brothers', there is no evidence that she ever existed. Jan Van Eyck's output was large. He is considered one of the great masters of the art of painting on account of his inventiveness, his severe technique, his power of imagination, and his understanding of people.

Vasari, Giorgio (1511-74)

Italian painter, architect and art historian, born at Arezzo, died in Florence. He is best known for his *Lives of the Most Eminent Painters, Sculptors and Architects*. This is an invaluable work containing a great deal of information about painting in the fourteenth, fifteenth and sixteenth centuries. As a painter himself, Vasari began his career in Michelangelo's workshop. Illness forced him to abandon painting for a while, but this did not stop him from furthering his study of architecture. He took up painting again in Rome in 1542, and executed a *Descent from the Cross* which is now in the Vatican. As an architect he was responsible for alterations to several churches in Florence, and he also built the Uffizi Gallery. He designed a chapel in Arezzo and painted its frescoes. He died in Florence before he was able to complete the decoration, commissioned by the Duke of Florence, of Santa Maria del Fiore. Vasari's *Lives* reveal his wide learning and his profound critical sense. He devoted a great deal of time—and money—to their composition. The book first appeared in 1550, and since then a dozen editions have been published in Italy.

Veneziano, Domenico (1400-61)

Italian painter of whom too little is known. Although his name means 'the Venetian' it is not certain that he came from Venice. In 1438, he was working in Perugia, where he decorated the vestibule of the Casa Baglioni with a series of twenty-five male portraits. Between 1435 and 1439 he painted *Il Vecchio* in the Sant'Egidio chapel in Santa Maria Novella, Florence, a work that has since disappeared. It is possible that he was assisted by his pupil, Piero della Francesca. Only two of Veneziano's works are now known: the *Madonna and Saints* in the Uffizi, the main panel of the St Bardi altar-piece; and the *Carnesecchi Madonna* in the National Gallery. These works prove that Domenico Veneziano studied painting in Florence.

Vivarini, Antonio (1415-76/84)

Italian painter, born in Murano. He founded the Murano school, which was an offshoot of the Venetian school. Little is known about his life. His existence is largely proved by the fact that he signed his works. These include a charming *Adoration of the Magi* in the Kaiser Friedrich Museum, Berlin, and a *Coronation of the Virgin* and an *Annunciation*, both now in the Accademia, Venice.

Witz, Conrad (*ca* 1400-47)

Swiss painter, born at Rottweil in Germany, died in Basle or Geneva. During the first half of the fifteenth century, the sculptors of the Burgundy School had a great influence on the painters of Southern Germany, whose most brilliant representatives were Conrad Witz and Stephan Lochner. The figures in Witz' paintings are often imitated from sculpture, and it is possible that he took the works of Claus Sluter as his models. Witz arrived in Basle in 1431, the year in which the Council of Basle was opened. Here he married, and had five children. His masterpiece is the *Heilsspiegel Altar-piece*, dating from 1435. Panels from this polyptych are now to be found in museums in Basle, Berlin and Dijon. François de Mies, Bishop of Geneva, who attended the Council of Basle, commissioned Witz to paint the main altar-piece for Geneva Cathedral, and this he did in 1444. This is his second greatest work, and is known as the *St Peter Altar-piece*. Its principal panel depicts *The Miraculous Draught of Fishes*. From the same period dates *Sts Catherine and Magdalen*, now in the Musée des Beaux-Arts, Strasbourg.

Wolgemut, Michael (1434-1519)

German painter and draughtsman, born and died in Nuremberg. Wolgemut was Hans Pleydenwurff's pupil and assistant, and was regarded as one of the greatest painters of his day. His masterpiece, the altar-piece which he painted for the church of Our Lady, Zwickau, dates from 1479. From 1486 to 1490, he had Albert Dürer as a pupil. Several art historians have asserted that some of the works attributed to Wolgemut were in fact painted by his pupils, for example, the Perinzdorfer altar-piece, which should perhaps be ascribed to his son-in-law, Wilhelm Pleydenwurff (Wolgemut had married Hans Pleydenwurff's widow). Wolgemut also produced wood engravings. With Wilhelm Pleydenwurff he illustrated several books, including Hartmann Schedel's *Weltchronik*, which was published *ca* 1491-4. There are paintings by Witz, or at least from his workshop, in the churches of Crailsheim, Hersbruck, Nuremberg and Schwabach, and also in the museums of Munich and Compiègne.